HABIT STACKING

By Ian Kennedy

Copyright © 2017 by Ian Kennedy

All Rights Reserved. This document is geared towards providing exact and reliable information in regards to the topic and issue covered. The publication is sold with the idea that the publisher is not required to render accounting, officially permitted, or otherwise, qualified services. If advice is necessary, legal or professional, a practiced individual in the profession should be ordered.

- From a Declaration of Principles which was accepted and approved equally by a Committee of the American Bar Association and a Committee of Publishers and Associations.

In no way is it legal to reproduce, duplicate, or transmit any part of this document in either electronic means or in printed format. Recording of this publication is strictly prohibited and any storage of this document is not allowed unless with written permission from the publisher. All rights reserved.

The information provided herein is stated to be truthful and consistent, in that any liability, in terms of inattention or otherwise, by any usage or abuse of any policies, processes, or directions contained within is the solitary and utter responsibility of the recipient reader. Under no circumstances will any legal responsibility or blame be held against the publisher for any reparation, damages, or monetary loss due to the information herein, either directly or indirectly.

Respective authors own all copyrights not held by the publisher.

The information herein is offered for informational purposes solely, and is universal as so. The presentation of the information is without contract or any type of guarantee assurance.

The trademarks that are used are without any consent, and the publication of the trademark is without permission or backing by the trademark owner. All trademarks and brands within this book are for clarifying purposes only and are the owned by the owners themselves, not affiliated with this document.

Disclaimer and Terms of Use: The Author and Publisher has strived to be as accurate and complete as possible in the creation of this book, notwithstanding the fact that he does not warrant or represent at any time that the contents within are accurate due to the rapidly changing nature of the Internet. While all attempts have been made to verify information provided in this publication, the Author and Publisher assumes no responsibility for errors, omissions, or contrary interpretation of the subject matter herein.

Any perceived slights of specific persons, peoples, or organizations are unintentional. In practical advice books, like anything else in life, there are no guarantees of results. Readers are cautioned to rely on their own judgment about their individual circumstances and act accordingly.

This book is not intended for use as a source of legal, medical, business, accounting or financial advice. All readers are advised to seek services of competent professionals in the legal, medical, business, accounting, and finance fields.

TABLE OF CONTENTS

Introduction 5

Chapter 1: The importance of habits 7

Chapter 2: Goals and habits: The yin and yang of success 12

Chapter 3: How habits are formed 15

Chapter 4: The nine most important habits that can change your life 20

Chapter 5: What is habit stacking? 29

Chapter 6: Building your own habit stacks 34

INTRODUCTION

Habits are a perfect example of those little things that we tend to take for granted because they are so familiar and routine. We hardly pay them any attention, unmindful of the fact that they have such a huge impact on our lives.

Stop for a moment and consider what you paid attention to today. Perhaps it was something work-related, like an important task that you had to do or a deadline that you had to beat. Or maybe what you remember about today is a particular conversation with your boss, spouse, or child. Or perhaps you were preoccupied with something you heard on the news (or through the grapevine?), or an email you got that surprised you. A hundred and one things can command our attention every day, and they hardly ever include our little habits.

Yet our habits matter greatly. They affect every aspect of our lives: our work, finances, relationships, health and happiness. The ease – or difficulty— with which we accomplish our work, relate with our peers or superiors, accomplish daily tasks, achieve our health and fitness goals, is very significantly influenced by our habits.

Habits can, in fact, spell the difference between success and failure in life. This is implied in the words of the famous Chinese philosopher Confucius when he said, "Men's natures are alike; it is their habits that separate them." He meant that what sets people apart, what distinguishes one person from another, is their habits. We'd like to be a little more blunt and say that habits are what separate successful men from those who aren't doing as well.

This idea is echoed by another famous philosopher, Aristotle, who said: "We are what we repeatedly do. Excellence then, is not an act, but a habit." Of course, we want to be excellent, and we want to succeed. We want the good things in life. We want our goals and dreams to become real. And because we want these, we need to pay closer attention to our habits. Obviously, there are habits that lead to success and happiness, and there are other habits that are detrimental to us. We'd like to cultivate habits of the first type, and discard those of the second type.

If you've ever wanted to create new habits and stop old ones that aren't serving you well, this book will help you do so. Here, we will first talk about habits in general and why they are so important. Then we will discuss habit stacking and how it can help to make your life so much easier and happier. We will also look at mini-habits that you can include in your daily routine to get you started living a better life. We'll talk about very useful and practical information about habits that you can immediately put to good use.

CHAPTER I:
THE IMPORTANCE OF HABITS

If we study the lives of great men, we will discover that their habits account for much of their success. Many business moguls, self-made millionaires, historical figures, famous celebrities, powerful politicians and exceptional athletes exemplify the power of habits. For them, the secret to success are certain habits that they have cultivated through the years. These are habits related to how they work, apply their skills, deal with other people, and use their time.

For example, the famous author Stephen King has the habit of writing at least ten pages every single day of the year, even on holidays. He never broke this habit, and the result is that he has become one of the most prolific writers of our time.

Another example is Benjamin Franklin, who is well-known for being exceptionally hard-working. He would wake up very early and work doggedly throughout the day. A habit that he always kept was to ask himself before starting to work (at around 5 a.m.), "What good shall I do today?" At the end of his workday (at around 10 p.m.), he would again ask himself, "What good have I done today?" This habit helped to ensure that he used his time as productively as possible.

Habits such as these certainly help a lot to make a person become successful at what he does. But, on the flipside, habits can also contribute to failure and loss. An obvious example of a destructive habit is alcoholism or substance abuse. Many famous people have fallen prey to this habit, contributing to their downward spiral, and even to their death in some cases. An example among many is Marilyn Monroe, who long struggled with substance abuse until she died from an overdose of barbiturates.

But we don't have to look at the lives of the famous (and infamous) to illustrate the importance and power of habits. In our own lives, we can see how some habits of ours may be contributing to our happiness and success, and how other habits are causing us pain and problems. Take a moment to reflect on some of your own habits. Which ones would you like to continue because they are serving you well, and which ones would you like to stop because they are keeping you from reaching your goals?

HOW HABITS LEAD TO SUCCESS

Actions are what bring about results. Dreaming, setting goals, planning, visualizing, and thinking about the future are important, but none of these can actually produce results. The same can be said for inspiration, vision, motivation, and even great ideas and intelligence. They are important, but they are not enough. Only concrete action can make things happen. Or more precisely, *steady* and *consistent* action is what makes goals happen. What we consistently and *habitually* do is what brings success.

Let's look at an example. Suppose you want to lose weight, like a lot of people do. You are very highly motivated, and you can clearly visualize what you'll look like and feel once you've reached your target weight. You do your homework by studying many diets and exercise programs. You finally choose a particular program to follow, and you're very eager to get started. You are to go on a low-carb diet for two weeks, and do cardio and resistance workouts in five days of each week. On the first day, you struggle a bit, but you feel strong and confident that you can continue with your new program. On Days 2 and 3, you keep on with the program, but you're now having a harder time. On Day 4, you continue to struggle, but you still stick with the diet and exercise. On Day 5, you can no longer stand it and so you eat ... a lot. Now you're back to square one. Or perhaps you're actually heavier now than before, because you binged and probably gained more weight than you have lost.

Does this story sound familiar? It should, because it has been the actual, frustrating experience of a lot of people.

In contrast, if you slowly but surely cultivated the habits of eating and exercising sensibly and healthily, over many weeks and months, then you probably won't have to experiment with yo-yo dieting. Because you were more consistent with your actions, you would then see concrete, positive results.

Good, sensible habits aren't very hard to cultivate, but you'll need to work on them, consistently. Once they become ingrained in you as habit, then you won't have to exert as much effort to continue doing them. You now do them automatically, easily, naturally. This makes life so much easier because you don't feel like you're working so hard. You're accomplishing your goals and getting things done, without sweating it. That's the beauty of habits.

THE COMFORT OF HABITS

Habits don't only make it easy for us to accomplish things that need to be done. They also reduce stress, and they bring a certain amount of calm and solace in stressful situations. There is comfort and reassurance in doing the familiar and routinary, and this is helpful in a lot of situations.

Consider the typical doctor in a typical E.R. environment. Despite the chaos and threat of injury and death all around him, he is able to stay calm and focused. He is able to calmly and competently attend to his patients, no matter how serious their injuries may be, and no matter how stressful the situation becomes. He is able to do this because it has become habitual for him to provide the necessary care in this type of environment. He is used to it. He does what he needs to do automatically and easily, without feeling the stress that someone new to the situation would undoubtedly feel.

Under extreme emotional stress, routines and habits provide a calming safety net. Thus, when something terrible happens, such as the death of a loved one, or the destruction of one's home due to a calamity, we can find solace in the reassuring habits of our everyday life. Returning to our routines can help us heal emotional wounds and deal more easily with trauma or pain.

ACTIONS MAKE THE MAN

Have you noticed how people's habitual actions become the labels that other people judge them by? Someone may say, "Oh, he's such a liar." Or, "she's the one who always arrives late, isn't she?" And, "Don't take him seriously, he's a regular Casanova!" While these may be snap judgments, they illustrate the fact that a person's actions—more than just his words or looks—determine how he is perceived by other people.

Clearly, for good or bad, our repetitive actions become who we are to the world. But habits go beyond just that; they also help define who we truly are. Our habits determine if we are successful or not, and if we are happy with our lives or not. They influence our health, the state of our finances, our relationships, and practically every aspect of our lives. If we repeatedly perform actions that lead to our success and happiness, we'll have those things eventually. Conversely, if we repeatedly do actions that lead to our harm or ruin, then we'll have that too.

Sean Covey, author and expert on habits, succinctly states, "We become what we repeatedly do." This is by no means a new truism. Hundreds of years earlier, the poet John Dryden made the same observation: "We first make out habits, then our habits make us."

If you'll examine your own life objectively, you will come to conclusion that you've arrived at this point where you are now as a result of your past actions. Your circumstances at this moment are dictated to a large degree by what you did yesterday, last week, last month, and last year. Your life now, and you as well, are a product of your past actions and habits. The present state of your health, finances, relationships, work, and so on—this is the outcome of your past actions and habits.

If you are happy with how things are now, then that's excellent. But if you are unhappy or dissatisfied, or if you want to change certain aspects of your life, then do something about your habits. Change them to bring about the change that you desire.

CHAPTER 2: GOALS AND HABITS: THE YIN AND YANG OF SUCCESS

Habits, while very important, are just one side of the success coin. On the other side are *goals*. Together, goals and habits ensure success and fulfillment. Thus, while this book is primarily about habits, we would be remiss if we didn't talk a bit about the value of goals and goal setting.

Goals will point you to the right direction, but it is habits that will get you where you want to go. If you have goals, but don't have the habits to support them, then you probably won't achieve those goals. On the other hand, if you have habits, but don't have the right goals, then you'll get somewhere, but it's not certain if that's where you really want to be.

Clearly, goals without habits aren't ideal. Neither are habits without goals. One without the order is likely to produce frustration and failure. Thus, it makes sense that you should give enough attention to both goals and habits.

If you are intent on making changes to improve your life, you should begin by setting goals properly. Then you can proceed to form the habits that will lead to the achievement of those goals.

HOW TO SET GOALS

Like most people, you already have some goals in mind. They may not be very clearly defined, but you know what you want from life, more or less. If you're like everyone else, you want to be happy, financially stable, gainfully employed, and maybe have a family of your own or be in a committed relationship. Some people have big dreams—of becoming very rich and influential, or of changing the world in some major way. You may be like that, or you may have more modest ambitions.

Whatever your persuasion is, we suggest that if you want real results, you should spend some time to really think about your goals. Clarify what they are, spell them out, and write them down. It's useful to have clear goals so that you'll know exactly what to do with your life. This helps to ensure that you won't waste precious time and effort. It also gives you direction, meaning and motivation.

To help you set your goals properly, keep these general guidelines in mind:

- Set goals that reflect your true desires, passion, values and personality. You should have goals that *you* believe in, and that *you* truly want. They shouldn't be other people's goals for you; they should be your own.

- Put your goals in writing. This clarifies them, and makes them "official." You can start doing this by first listing down goals that you care about, as they come to mind. Then cross out the goals which upon further reflection you don't really want, as well as those that aren't achievable or realistic, and those that don't reflect your personality and values.

- Use the S.M.A.R.T. method of setting goals. This means that your goals should be Specific, Measurable, Attainable, Relevant, and Time-bound.

- Create both short-term and long-term goals. The short-term goals can support the long-term ones, but those two could also be totally independent and separate from one another.

- Don't stop at setting goals. Once you've done that, you should formulate an action plan—however rudimentary—that outlines how you can make those goals become reality.

CHAPTER 3:
HOW HABITS ARE FORMED

The thing with habits is that they're hard to break. Once ingrained in us, a habit is very hard to discontinue. We continue doing it again and again even though we may know that it isn't doing us any good. An example is a smoker who struggles to quit. The longer he has had the habit, the harder it is for him to stop.

On the positive side, a good habit is also very hard to break. Thus, someone who has been eating healthily for years will probably continue to do so for the rest of his life. Another person who has been doing yoga or some workout every morning right after waking up, habitually, will likely continue this healthy custom for years and years.

So, a question that interests us now is: How do we form habits? We'll discuss this process a bit because it is very useful. Once we understand how habits are developed, we can use this knowledge to form new *good* habits and break some *bad* habits that we may already have.

THE ANATOMY OF A HABIT

Habit formation involves a cycle consisting of three elements, or the so-called *3 Rs*. These three are: *Reminder*, *Routine*, and *Reward*.

The Routine is the habit, behavior or action.

The Reminder is the cue that triggers the action.

And the Reward is the sense of benefit or fulfillment derived from doing the action.

Let's look at an example, say, the habit of drinking coffee early in the morning. The Reminder or cue may be that you are hungry and thirsty right after waking up. There has been no food in your body for several hours, and you now crave something to eat. And so you drink coffee, and this is the Routine. The Reward is feeling full and energized right after drinking coffee. Your sleepiness is gone, and you feel ready to face the new day. You like how this feels, and that is the Reward.

When this loop is repeated many, many times, it becomes a habit. You do the action automatically, without really consciously thinking about it, as if you are on autopilot. And there will come a time when you won't even need a Reminder nor a very good Reward for you to continue doing the action. You just do it, out of—you guessed it—habit.

THE 21-DAY MYTH

How long does it take for a habit to form? You may have heard that it takes about three weeks or 21 days. Others say that it takes up to 28 days. We aren't sure where these numbers come from, but the common belief is that when you've been doing something over and over again for three to four weeks, you will develop it as a habit.

Scientific research says otherwise, sort of. Findings from experiments reveal that it takes an *average* of 66 days for a habit to be fully formed. But the same experiments also showed that some habits do take a shorter time to form. For instance, the habit of drinking a glass of water after breakfast became automatic for majority of the subjects after about 20 days. The habit of doing sit-ups in the morning took much longer – 84 days – to take hold. Perhaps the difficulty of the action influences the length of time needed for that action to become habitual. There is also some variance from person to person. Some people develop certain habits faster than others do.

What is certain is that it takes many days to form a habit—66 days on average, as mentioned earlier.

It is also interesting to note that missing a day or two does not seem to affect habit formation significantly. Thus, you can miss out or slip for one day when trying to develop a habit, but it won't hamper your progress.

HOW TO START A NEW HABIT AND QUIT AN OLD HABIT

You can use the concept of the 3 Rs when trying to develop a new habit. Once you've identified an action (Routine) that you'd like to adopt, create or identify possible Reminders that you can use to lead to that action. Also create or identify some Rewards that will make the action worth doing for you.

For instance, you may want to start the habit of going to bed at a specific time, such as maybe 9:00 p.m. Create a loop of 3 Rs for this habit. You already have the habit as the Routine, so you'll need to create the Reminder and the Reward. The Reminder can be things that lead immediately to you getting in bed and sleeping. These could be preparatory actions such as brushing your teeth, putting on your night clothes, turning off the lights, and so on. All these can serve as triggers or cues leading to the Routine.

Reminders, in general, can actually come in the form of various things, including time, emotional state, location, other people, and other actions. For this example, the other things that can serve as Reminders are: it being 9:00 pm (time), you feeling tired or sleepy (emotional state), your bedroom (location), and maybe someone telling you good night (other people).

Meanwhile, the Reward can be waking up refreshed and ready to start the new day. Or you can actually reward yourself with a delicious breakfast or some other "treat" that will make you happy.

Similarly, when you want to quit a bad habit, the 3 Rs can also come into play. Find out the Reminders and Rewards attached to the habit that you want to stop, and try to eliminate or modify these so that you won't be repeating the action associated with them, namely, the bad habit.

Suppose you wish to quit smoking. That is the Routine you wish to stop. Let's say your Reminder (trigger) is when it's coffee break at work. At this time, you automatically go out to smoke. Related to this, another Reminder could be your feeling bored or maybe even stressed at work, which you wish to relieve by smoking. As for the Reward, perhaps you find smoking to be a welcome break from the monotony or stress of work. Maybe you also enjoy the chance to go outside and have a change of scenery.

With these Reminders and Rewards in mind, you can immediately find ways to eliminate the habit. You now know that during coffee break is a vulnerable time for you, so during this period, you should stay away from the smoking area and not have cigarettes within easy reach. Maybe you can arrange to be someplace else, doing something (like having a snack) that will take the place of smoking. You also know that you need a break from work or a change of scenery (this is the Reward or satisfaction that smoking gives you). You can derive this same reward from other things, such as by taking a short walk outside, or maybe playing a video game during your coffee break. These are some alternative actions that can take the place of smoking, which provide the same satisfaction or reward. You can to develop these as your new habits so that you can stop smoking.

The general idea is to disassociate the Reminders and Rewards from the Routine (bad habit). Link these with others things instead of the habit you wish to eliminate.

It sounds easy to do, but we know that in practice, it isn't. Breaking a bad habit requires hard work, consistency, and willpower.

Here are additional recommendations that can help you when you're trying to eliminate an undesirable habit:

- Enlist the help of another person, such as someone who is also trying to quit the same habit. You can hold one another accountable, motivate each other, and celebrate small victories together.

- Replace the bad habit with a new (good) habit. Some people believe that the only effective way to kick a habit is to replace it with another habit. Gum chewing can replace smoking, for example. Any enjoyable (and wholesome) hobby can be used as a substitute for a habit you wish to get rid of.

- Cut out the triggers. This is similar to removing the Reminders associated with the habit. Eliminate as much as possible all temptations that lead you to the action you wish to avoid. If you wish to stop eating junk food, remove them from your pantry and don't buy any more of them.

- Don't beat yourself up when you slip, but make sure you get up and try again. Because we're human and imperfect, it's alright to "fall of f the wagon" once in a while. Just don't use a failure as an excuse to stop trying altogether to quit a habit. Keep trying, again and again, no matter how often you fail.

- Penalize yourself when you slip, and reward yourself when you stay on track.

CHAPTER 4: THE NINE MOST IMPORTANT HABITS THAT CAN CHANGE YOUR LIFE

Given enough time, we can probably think of many helpful habits that we'd like to be able to practice every day. But realistically speaking, we can only focus on a handful of habits at any given time. It does take real effort and commitment to cultivate a habit, and so, if we wish to get good results, we must be selective in choosing which habits to work on.

Below is a list of some good habits worth cultivating. This list takes into account what psychologists and lifestyle gurus believe to be essential attitudes and actions that help to create a happy and meaningful life. The habits included aren't listed in any particular order. Feel free to choose any one of them, or a few, that you think can make a difference in your life.

HABIT #1: POSITIVE THINKING

The habit of thinking positively is an important one that can support the formation of other useful habits. It is therefore a very desirable habit and general attitude of mind to have. When you think positively and with optimism, you are naturally motivated to try out new things and work towards any goal. This frame of mind gives you added energy. It doesn't hurt that it also makes you an easier person to get along with. Naturally, everyone enjoys the company of a happy and optimistic person more than that of a dour or cynical individual.

Thinking positively also comes in handy when you're trying to get rid of bad habits. A bad habit, such as smoking or mindless overeating, can be very difficult to eliminate because it is so ingrained in the person. He can easily become discouraged and give up before even giving it a real try. But when he thinks positively, there's a greater chance that he will keep trying until he eventually conquers the habit.

To get into the habit of positive thinking, always look towards the bright side. Anticipate good results, and prepare to work hard for them. Also very importantly, watch out for negative thoughts. These can come from other people, but more often, they come from within your own self. Negative self-talk is very common, and psychologists say that it is a huge source of unhappiness for a lot of people. So try to catch yourself when negative thoughts strike. Here are some examples to be wary of:

- It's too difficult.
- I can't possibly do it.
- I'm too _____ (fat, thin, shy, young, old, short, tall, etc.) to be able to do it.
- What will people say?
- I'll just embarrass myself if I go through with it.
- It's a waste of time.
- It's not worth it.
- I'm not worth it.
- I'm not ready.

Whenever you think of these or other negative thoughts that resemble them, take a deep breath, and pause for a while. Ask yourself if those thoughts arise out of fear, laziness, a low self-esteem, or a natural resistance to change. Then simply refuse to believe in the negative thought and proceed with what you were planning to do. Tell yourself that you can do it, and that it will be done.

HABIT #2: KEEPING A GRATITUDE JOURNAL

A gratitude journal is simply a notebook where you record things that you are grateful for every day. You write on it something that made you happy that day. It can be a kind gesture that someone did for you, an event that took place, a state of things, a certain feeling, a possession or object you value, an experience—anything that you are grateful for. Even if nothing special actually happened on a given day, you can still think of many things to be grateful for, such as your health, the good weather, having friends and family that care for you, the birds singing outside, the smell of a freshly mowed lawn, and so on.

The point of having a gratitude journal is to focus on the positive things in your life. When you do this habitually, you will develop an attitude of positivity, optimism, hope and gratitude. Having this mindset will make you a happier person, regardless of what's actually happening in your life.

When bad or sad things happen, you can read some entries in your gratitude journal and be reminded that life still has so much to offer.

A notebook that you write on is the best way to keep a gratitude journal. But should you wish to, you can use apps on your mobile phone or computer that function as an electronic gratitude journal.

HABIT #3: ELIMINATING THE NON-ESSENTIAL

This means living simply and cutting out extraneous activities and objects. To do this, first identify what is essential to you, what is most important, or what gives you the greatest happiness. Then eliminate everything else.

Another way of going about it is putting everything through a litmus test. For example, ask yourself if an activity is essential, important, or joy-giving. If it isn't, then don't do it. Extend the same test to other things in your life, such as relationships, possessions, emails and social media, and so on. Before making a purchase, apply the test. Before committing to a social engagement, apply the same test. Then act accordingly.

Make simplifying your life a habit. When you do so, you can really focus on the important things. And you will also have immensely more time and energy for them. You can then build the life that you really want.

HABIT #4. EXERCISING

Are you shaking your head right now and wondering how exercising is one of the top habits to cultivate? You shouldn't, because there are a lot of reasons why exercise is very important. Here are some of them:

- Exercise keeps you healthy.

- It prevents or cures depression and other mood disorders, as well as a host of diseases and medical conditions.

- It makes you happy.

- It fosters optimism and positive thinking.

- It makes you feel good about yourself, boosting your self-confidence.

- It relieves stress.
- It clears your mind.
- It is relaxing.
- It makes you sleep better.
- It promotes creativity and mental health.

As such, do try to have some form of exercise as a habit. It can be something as simple as talking a walk or a jog every other day. Or you can join a gym or a sports club. It will do wonders for your health, and you'll be a much happier person too.

HABIT #5. SINGLE-TASKING

This may sound unfamiliar to you, but it's just the opposite of multi-tasking. Single-tasking simply means working on only one thing (a single task) at a time. It is life-changing, and it results in a tremendous boost in productivity. Studies reveal that contrary to popular belief, multitasking isn't an efficient method of getting things done in the workplace. A person is more effective and efficient when he does only one piece of work at a time, rather than when he juggles several tasks together.

When a person single-tasks, he also experiences less stress. Offices and workplaces where people single-task are calmer, happier and more efficient spaces.

Another benefit of single-tasking is that it encourages focus and mindfulness. Because the person is doing only one thing, he can focus completely on it, increasing the likelihood that he'll do an excellent job. In addition to performing excellently, he also learns to cultivate the habit of mindfulness, or being attuned to the here and now. This, in itself, can be a simple form of meditation with many wonderful benefits to the person practicing it.

HABIT #6: SPENDING MONEY ON EXPERIENCES, NOT MATERIAL THINGS

Possessions come and go, break and fall, go out of trend, and so on. On the other hand, experiences turn into memories that you can cherish for the rest of your life. If you want the secret to happiness, this is it: Spend money on experiences, not possessions.

This claim is backed up by extensive psychological research. Research findings show that material possessions do not provide life-long happiness because of three things:

1. There are always new possessions to be had.

2. Our expectations are ever increasing.

3. We are always comparing our possessions to what somebody else has.

In other words, material possessions will always disappoint us.

Experiences, meanwhile, have the power to inspire us, even after they're done. They become a part of our identity, shaping us to become better versions of ourselves. They are also more special because they are fleeting, which gives us a sense of anticipation and excitement for what is yet to come. In addition, your experiences are unique to you and you alone. Even if you travel with a friend, your experience of that trip is still different from his. Therefore, comparisons do not really matter.

While new and better versions of gadgets, cars and other material possessions are created, your experiences will remain unique and special to you.

HABIT #7. BEING KIND

Yes, you're reading it right. Kindness is a habit, and one that every person should cultivate.

Being kind means doing a kind act for someone, anyone. It can be for a friend, a family member, co-worker, or a total stranger. It doesn't have to involve giving away money or something with a monetary value. It just means being compassionate and friendly. It can mean volunteering in a charitable event, lending a helping hand, patting someone in the back for a job well done, or listening to a person who needs to vent. Opportunities for kind acts are not hard to find. They could be right inside your home or your workplace. Grab the chance to be kind whenever you can, and you won't just be benefitting the other person. You'll also feel good, and you'll feel connected to another human being. That's always a lovely thing.

Work on being kind as you would on any other habit that you'd like to cultivate. Every day, take every chance you get to be kind to someone else. After a while, you'll witness profound changes happening in your life. For one thing, you'll feel a deeper kind of peace and calmness. People will react to you differently and—not surprisingly—treat you more kindly. What you give out will really come back to you. That's karma.

HABIT #8: MAKING LISTS

This is a practical habit that will increase your productivity and keep you organized. Lists are useful not only as visual reminders, but also to help you to plan ahead and clarify your priorities. When you list something down, that means you have given it some thought, and that you consider it to be important.

You can make lists of many things, such as tasks that you need to do, grocery items or supplies that you need to buy, people you need to contact or buy gifts for (on holidays such as Christmas), and interesting ideas that come to you at unexpected moments. It is therefore a good practice (another habit to learn!) to always bring with you a small notebook where you can write down these lists and reminders, at any time that an idea or item to include occurs to you. If you wish, you can use your smart phone to jot down your lists. There are many apps for list-making that you can download and use.

Another benefit of making lists is that it gives you the satisfaction of crossing out items that have been completed. There is a simple pleasure in this that encourages greater productivity and that just makes you feel good about yourself.

HABIT #9: WAKING UP EARLY

Each person's schedule is different, so it's difficult to pin down a specific time that everyone would consider as "early." It is ideal if you can wake up before or at sunrise and enjoy the quietude of that time. Everyone else is still asleep, and the world is quiet and at peace. It is a wonderful, beautiful time to do something meaningful, or to just enjoy quietly. However, if you cannot get up this early, then just consider waking up at least 30 minutes earlier than your usual waking-up time.

Think of this habit as allowing yourself an extra 30 minutes or so of the day for special me-time. You can do with this time whatever you wish, but we suggest that it be something meaningful or special. If you are a prayerful person, use this time to pray, meditate or practice gratefulness.

If you are a sporty person, this time is perfect for an outdoor run or yoga/tai-chi session (you'll enjoy seeing the sunrise as a bonus). If you prefer to use this time to get some important work done, then go ahead and use it to plan your day or to make a list of the tasks that you want to accomplish.

Doing something useful, beautiful, or meaningful first, right after you wake up, will set the tone for the rest of the day. It is a great start to what probably would be a great day.

CHAPTER 5:
WHAT IS HABIT STACKING?

Habit stacking is a simple and surefire way to create good habits. The idea behind it is straightforward: take simple, easy-to-do actions (we call them *mini-habit*), and "stack" them together to create a routine. To stack means to pile up neatly, or to put several things together, one on top of another. Necessarily, you should include only easy and quick tasks in habit stacking. Big and difficult tasks aren't "stackable," and so they aren't to be used in habit stacking.

The truth is that you may already be doing habit stacking right now. Think of your morning routine. This probably includes brushing your teeth, taking a shower, having coffee or tea, and scanning the headlines on the newspaper. There's even a sequence on how you stack these small habits together. One small habit naturally follows another, almost serving as a cue or trigger for the next habit in the routine. You do this morning routine every day, without much thought or effort. This is a common example of habit stacking. It doesn't seem complicated, does it?

An important key to habit stacking is to take small tasks that don't take up too much time or effort. The entire stack or routine, meaning all the mini-habits put together, shouldn't take longer than 30 minutes or so. That means that each mini-habit should roughly take 5 to 10 minutes, more or less.

Because a habit stack isn't time-consuming, you can easily squeeze one, two or even three or more stacks in your daily schedule. It won't create any disruption in your usual day, but if you consistently do it, the returns will be tremendous.

Another key element in a habit stack is that one mini-habit serves as the Reminder or cue for the next mini-habit. For this to happen, the sequence in which the small tasks are to be done has to be kept consistent. Always do the first mini-habit first, and the second next, and then the third, and so on. Don't switch them around.

HOW TO HABIT STACK

There are rules in building a habit stack that you should follow to create your own personal routines. These will help ensure that you form a routine that is doable, and that you can easily incorporate in your current daily schedule.

The rules are as follows:

1. ATTACH THE STACK TO AN EXISTING HABIT.

The simplest way to remember a stack is to do it right before or after a habit that you already have. This should be something you do without fail, every single day—like eating, brushing your teeth, or checking your phone. This is important because you're going to piggyback on this habit by creating what's called an "if-then statement."

If-then statements can help you stick with a goal and, more importantly, will prevent those times when you want to skip a day. The idea here is to identify an *existing* habit then create a specific action you'll complete immediately before or after this routine.

For instance, you could create if-then statements like:

- "I will start my habit stacking routine right after *I get out of the bathroom first thing in the morning.*"

- "I will floss my teeth right before *I brush them in the evening.*"
- "I will give 'one last look' before *turning left while driving.*"
- "I will pack my gym bag right after *I put on my clothes for the day.*"
- "I will eat a salad right before *my dinner.*"

As you can see, each if-then plan is attached to an existing behavior (the action in italics).

2. COMPLETE EACH MINI-HABIT IN FIVE MINUTES OR LESS (USUALLY).

Five minutes is just the general rule; you are allowed some leeway here. This means that you can go (slightly) beyond five minutes if the mini-habit is important enough to you, and if it takes that much time to do.

3. THE ENTIRE ROUTINE SHOULD TAKE THIRTY MINUTES.

We like to put a cap on how long a habit stack takes because most people already lead busy lives. They don't have a lot of free time. In fact, according to many life coaches, people on average are willing (or able) to devote no more than 30 minutes each day to work on self-improvement. We'd like to use those 30 minutes then as a reasonable target time to complete one habit stacking routine.

Again, this number of minutes is to be taken as a general rule of thumb. You can go slightly below or over it, depending on how busy you are, and on how many tasks you wish to include in the stack.

4. BUILD DAILY, WEEKLY, AND MONTHLY STACKS.

Some habits don't require daily effort. Instead, they are best completed on a weekly or monthly interval. For instance, certain actions only require the occasional "checkup," like reviewing your credit card purchases, inspecting your smoke detectors, and checking your tire pressure. Each is important, but it's better to schedule these actions on a weekly or monthly basis.

5. EACH MINI-HABIT SHOULD BE A COMPLETE ACTION.

There should be an obvious starting and stopping point. In other words, you should avoid habits where you could easily do more of it if you had time (like exercising, writing, or anything related to your job). It's better to schedule these activities for a different part of the day when you can devote more time to them.

For example, there isn't a lot of value in cramming five minutes of exercise into a habit stack because it won't give you the full benefit of improved fitness and strength. Instead, a better use of your time is to pack your gym bag for the day or to record a workout from the day before. Each action supports your larger habits and has a clear starting and stopping point.

6. PICK SIMPLE-TO-DO TASKS FOR YOUR HABIT STACK.

Each mini-habit should be easy to complete without requiring a lot of brainpower. The idea here is to do it quickly and then immediately move on to the next action. If you need time to complete a series of steps, then perhaps you should schedule this habit for another time in the day.

Remember, each activity should only require a single step, or maybe two steps, to complete. Examples include making a bed, packing a bag, preparing a smoothie, or updating your expenditures from the previous day.

7. START ONE HABIT STACK AT A TIME.

So that you won't be overwhelmed, build one, and only one, habit stack first and proceed to do it daily. Only after several days or weeks, when you feel that you've already cultivated this routine as a habit, should you make another habit stack to do. Go about the process easy, without hurrying, to ensure that you succeed building good habits for life.

CHAPTER 6: BUILDING YOUR OWN HABIT STACKS

There are a number of mini-habits, or small tasks, that we highly recommend that you include in your habit stacks. While these are simple and easy-to-do actions, they can make a lot of difference in your life when done repeatedly, daily, as habits.

Pick only a few of these mini-habits to include in your first habit stack. As mentioned earlier, you shouldn't attempt to start two or more habit stacks together. Start easy by building just one routine first, and only after that has become automatic and habitual for you should you build and work on your next stacks.

By all means, include tasks that you think of, that will be useful to you, even though they may not be found in the lists below.

MINI-HABITS THAT CAN HELP IMPROVE YOUR CAREER

1. Schedule your day early in the morning. List down the tasks you want to complete by the end of the day. Be realistic as you do so, meaning that you shouldn't list down more than what you can actually do.

2. Prioritize your list in #1 by identifying your Top 3 tasks for the day. These three are the most important, and they therefore are the "must-dos" for the day. This focuses your attention and helps you to schedule your time as well.

3. Start each workday by doing the hardest or most important task(s) first. You have the greatest amount of energy and focus early in the morning, so do what really matters first. You can do the less important tasks later in the day.

4. Make a difficult or large task more manageable by breaking it down into smaller tasks.

5. Remove distractions, such as social media, before starting to work. Put calls on hold if you need to.

6. Clean up your desktop. Remove clutter so that you can focus on your work.

7. Play quiet music in the background to improve your focus at work.

8. Make one new business connection or contact each day.

9. Dress for success.

10. Reward yourself whenever you complete a difficult or milestone task.

11. Track and log the time you allot for certain tasks. This will make you see how you spend your time, and allow you to make any changes if necessary.

12. At the end of the day, make a "done list." It's simply a list of the tasks that you completed that day. It is a way to review your day, and to allow yourself that well-earned feeling of satisfaction for having accomplished that much.

MINI-HABITS RELATED TO BUDGET AND FINANCE

1. Check your billing statements. You can spot any discrepancies that you need to report, if any. You can also see where your money goes, and become aware of your large purchases.

2. Conserve on your utilities. This means your electricity, phone, cable TV, water, heat, and so on. Avoid wastage. Turn off appliances that aren't in use. If you're not using something fully, such as your cable TV subscription, consider cutting it off.

3. Pack meals, snacks and coffee to work instead of buying them. This can help you to cut down on expenses, as well as make healthier food choices.

4. Track your daily expenses. Also track your weekly and monthly expenses.

5. Review your financial situation. You can do this by asking questions such as:

   - Do you have a savings plan?
   - What are your mandatory expenses?
   - Is there any spending habit that you can reduce or eliminate?
   - How much credit card debt do you have?
   - Do you have enough of an emergency fund?
   - How much interest are you earning on your savings?
   - How much are you spending (and saving) each month?
   - What are your spending triggers?

6. Review your budget. This enables you to see where your money actually goes. See if you can cut down on some expenses, especially on frivolous or impulse purchases. Then you can begin to create an organized approach to your finances. Believe it or not, this can be a great stress reliever.

7. Negotiate a lower price every time you make a purchase. As they say, you have nothing to lose, and everything to win if you try

to do this. It can be a win-win situation for both you and the salesman who is eager to make a sale.

8. Research well before making a major purchase. Compare prices. Avoid buying the first item you see that appears to meet the criteria you have in mind.

9. Use coupons. It's an easy way to reduce your spending. You might even enjoy collecting coupons like you would a hobby.

10. Carefully prepare your shopping lists. Consider if each item is really healthy or necessary. When you do get out to shop, don't buy anything that isn't on your lists.

MINI-HABITS TO BOOST YOUR HEALTH

1. Jump-rope. It's an aerobic exercise that most people can do, regardless of age or the state of their health. It can even be fun, reliving memories of childhood.

2. Do push-ups. You need to do resistance or weight training too, and push-ups are a good example of this. If you wish, you can do sit-ups at other times, or lift weights.

3. Meditate. This is a method of stress relief and relaxation that can be done anywhere, at any time. Try to do mindfulness meditation and deep breathing especially when you're idle, such as when you're in a queue or when waiting for something.

4. Practice good posture.

5. Keep a food journal. This will help you to spot patterns of eating that you may need to change to become a healthier person. This will be of great help especially if you need to lose some weight.

6. Take daily multivitamins. We know this is a must, but a lot of people neglect to do this. Adults need enough Vitamin C and

B complex especially. Women should be particularly careful that they get enough iron, folate, magnesium, and Vitamins A and E.

7. Do any seven- to ten-minute workout. You can mix it up, doing aerobic or cardio exercises at one time, and then resistance training at another time.

8. Prepare and drink a healthy smoothie.

9. Drink one glass of water every hour or so. The target is to drink a total of at least 2 liters of water every day.

10. Introduce a (new) healthy food item to your meals periodically.

11. Eliminate one unhealthy food from your diet periodically.

12. Track your daily steps and try to meet target numbers. A good initial target is 3,000 to 5,000 steps daily. You can increase this number as the weeks go by.

13. Weigh yourself regularly (daily, weekly, monthly).

14. Skip breakfast periodically, or don't eat anything before 10:00 am. You can do this every other day, or at least twice a week. This is helpful if you wish to lose some weight. Skipping any caloric food in the morning is a form of intermittent fasting that has been proven to produce many health benefits including weight loss.

MINI-HABITS FOR LEISURE

1. Learn something new: new information, a new language, a new hobby, etc. It is a pleasurable activity that also stimulates your brain. If possible, learn something new that isn't related to your line of work. You will enjoy its novelty and unfamiliarity.

2. Watch an inspiring video. You can find many of these on YouTube.

3. Read one chapter in a book, any book. This is great to do at night before going to sleep. It is preferable that you read a real, physical book instead of an ebook on your smartphone or tablet.

4. Listen to news highlights (on the TV or radio).

5. Learn a new word each day, and use it. There are some apps for mobile phones for this. Download one such app, or simply consult a dictionary and find an unfamiliar word.

6. Use an adult coloring book. This is a very enjoyable pastime that also provides stress relief.

7. Enjoy the outdoors. Take a walk, or just go outside to enjoy the sun or fresh air.

8. Do a crossword puzzle.

9. Sketch or doodle. Even if you're not good at sketching, give it a try. You may even discover that you want to learn to draw better. Definitely go for it.

10. Make a "bucket list" of things you'd like to do before you die. Go deep and ask yourself something that you'd really, really, really love to do, and will surely do if money, time or your health aren't a hindrance. It is pleasurable to just dream of these things, but who knows, they just might happen one day.

11. Try something new. It can be a new recipe, a new activity, a new drink, a new route to work. The possibilities are endless. Just try something you haven't done before.

MINI-HABITS TO KEEP YOU ORGANIZED

1. Make your bed. This is something that you can, and should, include in your morning routine. A neat bed can transform your bedroom, making it look very tidy and inviting. It also does something to your subconscious mind; it sends the message that you're ready to start the day, and that everything's in place.

2. Clear a table, such as your home office desk. Clutter is never good, messing up not only your physical space but also, very subtly, your mental and emotional state.

3. Fix a broken window (or anything at home that needs to be repaired).

4. Clean one refrigerator shelf.

5. Organize the contents of one drawer or cabinet.

6. Put loose paperwork in a file or drawer.

7. Find a place for every object you own, especially for those that tend to be scattered everywhere around house. You will avoid misplacing so many things and wasting time trying to find them.

8. Declutter your mobile phone. Remove apps and contacts that you don't really need or use anymore. Also erase messages, pictures, videos and other files that are just taking up unnecessary space.

9. Discard one item that you don't use anymore, or that you can donate to charity.

10. Jot down ideas as they come to you. Write down interesting ideas, big ones, even small ones that maybe you can use one day.

11. Say no to events, invitations or favors asked of you that you cannot comfortably fit in your schedule, or that you'd rather not do.

MINI-HABITS FOR BETTER RELATIONSHIPS

1. Contact one person on a dating site. You don't have to commit to a date right away. Just say hi and maybe start a conversation.

2. Send an encouraging or affectionate text message to someone close to you (a partner, family member or friend). This doesn't take much time or effort, but the other person will appreciate it.

3. Return a phone call or text message within 24 hours. Getting back to someone right away tells them that they are important to you.

4. Leave someone a thoughtful, caring note. Don't wait for special occasions to show people you care about that they matter to you.

5. Give someone a sincere compliment. That person will appreciate it, and it can even be just the right gesture at a moment that he or she really needs some cheering up or encouragement.

6. Hug someone. It will be good for you and for the other person. Just make sure you do with to someone you're close to.

7. Do something that gives you pleasure or happiness. Do not neglect to be good to yourself too. Taking care of yourself is important so that you can take care of others.

8. Introduce yourself to someone new. But don't do it mechanically. Try to form a connection, be interested in the other person. Who knows, you may be starting a friendship or relationship that you will come to cherish in the years to come.

9. Learn a new joke and tell it to someone. Everyone enjoys a good laugh. Be the one to introduce some light cheer especially when everyone needs a break from the monotony or stress of work.

10. Pause and reflect thoughtfully before commenting on a sensitive topic. Always try to be tactful and considerate.

11. Pause and reflect before saying anything while you're angry or emotional. Try to avoid saying things that you will regret later.

12. Research a fun activity that you can do with someone. And then do it when your schedule permits.

MINI-HABITS THAT CAN ENHANCE YOUR SPIRITUAL LIFE

1. Practice gratitude. Write an entry on your gratitude journal, or simply observe a moment of silence while you reflect on your many blessings. Even if you feel that you're going through a difficult time, you can still find many things to be thankful for.

2. Do a random act of kindness. It need not cost a single cent, but this act will do wonders to lift your spirit and someone else's. Little things like a simple smile to say hello, an encouraging word, or an offer to carry someone's heavy things, are always appreciated. If you are able to, you can also do something surprising like anonymously paying for the table next to you before leaving a restaurant. There are many opportunities to practice kindness. Grab them, and you'll feel as good as the person for whom you're doing the kind act.

3. Use positive affirmations. Here are some that you can use, but feel free to create your own:

   - "I will accomplish my goals and tasks today."
   - "I have full control of my life."
   - "I am loved."
   - "I am worthy of joy."
   - "I am alive and full of energy and positivity."

- "I can make a change in the world."
- "My life is brimming with abundance and blessings."

4. Practice deep breathing and relaxation.

5. Pray. No matter what your concept of God is, praying to a higher power is very calming and stress-relieving. It is also a source of strength and inspiration. It can help you through tough times, and make you more appreciative of your life at any moment.

6. Donate to a charitable organization. You can donate money, goods or your time and presence to a cause that you feel strongly about.

7. Drink a calming tea.

8. Practice creative visualization.

9. Walk mindfully. Wearing comfortable clothes and shoes, take a walk while focusing on the sensory messages that come to you. Listen, feel, hear, smell and see what's happening around you and in you. You can also focus on the movements of your feet and legs, or on the swinging of your arms. This is a practice that will train you to focus on the now and on what's real, instead of on thoughts, worries, plans, regrets, what-ifs and other creations of your mind.

10. Use aromatherapy. This ancient art of relaxing the mind, body and spirit continues to be used today because it is effective and easy to do. Our sense of smell is powerfully connected to the brain, bringing about many health benefits. Some good scents you can use are: rose, lavender, jasmine, lemon, tea tree, peppermint, chamomile, sandalwood and bergamot.

11. Do volunteer work.

12. Practice forgiveness and letting go. When thoughts about past

hurts and regrets come, breathe gently, close your eyes, and say: "I forgive you" or "I let go." Imagine you are letting go of the past, in the same manner that you would say goodbye to a friend. Then open your eyes, and immerse yourself in the present.

FINAL THOUGHTS ABOUT HABIT STACKING

Combine any of the simple, easy-to-do tasks enumerated above, or use little tasks that you think of, to make habit stacks that you can try out for several days or a few weeks and see if they're working well for you. If they are, you can perhaps adopt them as a lifelong practice.

You can make a habit stack suitable for the early morning right after waking up, and another one to do during your lunch break, and another for the evening. You can also create stacks that you can do at home, at work, in the gym, or at other places you frequent. You can even create habits stacks for specific purposes, such as for losing weight, for dating, or for increasing your productivity levels.

<u>As an example, here is a productivity stack that you can do:</u>

- Remove distractions before starting to work.
- Clean up your desktop by removing clutter.
- Identify your three most important tasks for the day.
- Do the most difficult task first.
- Play some background music to improve your focus.
- Track the time for your activities.
- Reward yourself for completing a difficult task.
- Write a "done list."

The whole stack will usually take 20 to 30 minutes.

It is important to keep in mind that you should go slowly, focusing on cultivating just one habit stack at a time. Only if you feel you can handle it, without being overwhelmed, should you add one or two more habit stacks.

For a lot of people who are new to habit stacking, the main obstacle they need to hurdle is to *begin*. You may feel like you want to postpone starting a habit stack until you feel more inspired or ready. You may also feel that you don't have the time for it. We tell you now that you just have to start, regardless of how you feel. You have to stop making excuses and start doing. That's the only way to do it, and *you* are the only person who can make that happen.

Remember that habits can spell success or failure in life. If you act now, you're choosing for yourself a better and happier future, one that you're actually *creating* right now with the habits that you're starting to cultivate.

www.ingramcontent.com/pod-product-compliance
Lightning Source LLC
Chambersburg PA
CBHW030058230526
45471CB00003B/1152